North American Wildlife from A to Z

Animal Kingdom ABCs

A Photo Journey Exploring the Fascinating Creatures of North America with Fun Facts for Kids Who Love Wild Animals

by Michele Renee Acosta

Published by
Just Because...Books
an imprint of
My Extra Umbrella

North American Wildlife from A to Z:
A Photo Journey Exploring the Fascinating Creatures of North America
with Fun Facts for Kids Who Love Wild Animals
Copyright © 2026 by Michele Renee Acosta

Library of Congress Cataloging-in-Publication Data is available.
Library of Congress Control Number: 2024922758

ISBN (hardcover): 979-8-89615-064-0
ISBN (paperback): 979-8-89615-004-6
ISBN (ebook–Kindle edition): 979-8-89615-011-4
ISBN (ebook–EPUB edition): 979-8-89615-071-8

Published by
Just Because...Books
an imprint of My Extra Umbrella
1968 South Coast Highway
Suite 891
Laguna Beach, California 92651
Publisher@MyExtraUmbrella.com

This is Book 4 in the *Animal Kingdom ABCs* series.

Books in the *Animal Kingdom ABCs* series can be read in any order.

Printed in Laguna Beach, California, U.S.A.

First Edition

Author's Note

Welcome to *North American Wildlife from A to Z*, a book that invites young children to embark on an exciting adventure through North America's diverse wildlife. This book, part of the *Animal Kingdom ABCs* series, is designed to introduce children to wildlife from across the North American continent in a way that's both fun and engaging. While it may look like a traditional ABC book, it goes far beyond teaching the alphabet. Instead, it's a window into the fascinating world of the animals and other wildlife that inhabit this unique part of the globe.

Each book in the series is organized alphabetically, which helps young pre-readers easily follow along and engage with the content. However, it's not about "learning the ABCs" in the usual sense. Rather, it's about sparking curiosity about wildlife and showing how vast and varied the animal kingdom can be, one letter at a time. Many of the wildlife names in this book—like *quail* and *uinta ground squirrel*—are not words typically found in a traditional ABC book. That's part of the fun! While these words may be challenging to pronounce, it's a great way for children to expand their vocabulary and learn about creatures they might never have encountered before. Note that no wildlife exists in North America that begins with the letter X. Rather than exclude a letter from the alphabet, I've offered the opportunity for children to use what they've learned about wildlife from this part of the world to imagine an animal with features needed to survive in the habitats and climates on this continent.

Before reading for the first time, I encourage you to have a conversation about the animals children might expect to see in a book about North American wildlife. Ask children to share what they already know about animals in general and North American animals in particular. At the end of the book, you'll find fun facts about North American wildlife, as well as critical-thinking questions designed to inspire deeper conversations. These questions are perfect for further exploration of the topic and for encouraging curiosity and a life-long love of learning.

Remember, the goal of this book is discovery and wonder. It's okay if the animal names are tricky— that's why I included helpful pronunciations and facts! This book, and the series as a whole, aims to offer children an opportunity to explore the natural world continent by continent, fostering a sense of adventure, awe, and connection to the animals with which we share this planet.

Thank you for joining me on this exciting adventure through North America's animal kingdom!

Happy exploring!

Michele Renee Acosta

A

American Black Bear

B

Bald Eagle

C

Coyote

Dall Sheep

E

Elk

F

Fox

G

Grizzly Bear

H

Hawk

Indigo Bunting

J

Jackrabbit

K

Kildeer

L

Lynx

M

Moose

N

North American Porcupine

O

Opossum

P

Pronghorn

Q

Quail

R

Raccoon

S

Skunk

T

Turkey

U

Uinta Ground Squirrel

Vulture

W

White-Tailed Deer

What would your animal eat?

Where would your animal live?

X

Name Your Animal!

X._____

Invent an animal that could live in the Rocky Mountains!

Y

Yellow-Bellied Marmot

Z

Zebra Swallowtail Butterfly

Would You Believe?

American Black Bears can climb trees using their strong curved claws, even as 600-pound adults!

Bald Eagles have vision four times sharper than humans and can spot prey from over a mile away.

Coyotes can adapt to cities and suburbs and even use crosswalks!

Dall Sheep use their curled horns to clash in headbutting contests that can last for hours.

Elk antlers can grow an inch a day in summer, faster than any other bone in the animal kingdom.

Foxes have excellent hearing. They can hear a mouse squeak from 100 feet away!

Grizzly Bears dig huge dens into hillsides to hibernate all winter long. While they sleep, their heart rate drops from about 84 beats per minute to as low as eight beats per minute.

Hawks can dive at speeds over 120 miles per hour to snatch prey mid-air.

Indigo Buntings aren't actually blue! Their feathers bend light in a way that makes them look blue.

Jackrabbits can leap 10 feet in a single bound to escape predators.

Killdeer pretend to have a broken wing to trick predators away from their nests.

Lynx have super-sharp hearing. Tufts on their ears may help them hear even better!

Moose are the largest members of the deer family. They can weigh over 1,500 pounds!

North American Porcupines have over 30,000 quills, each with tiny barbs that are hard to pull out.

Opossums are North America's only marsupial. And they're immune to most snake venom!

Pronghorn can run up to 55 miles per hour. That's faster than any other animal in North America.

Quail parents often form a line with their babies following behind like a tiny train.

Raccoons are expert problem-solvers! They can even open jars and doors with their five finger-like toes.

Skunks warn predators by stomping before spraying. And they only spray when they really have to because it takes time to make more!

Turkeys can fly short distances at up to 55 miles per hour!

Uinta Ground Squirrels spend up to nine months a year hibernating underground!

Vultures can glide for hours without flapping their wings by riding warm air currents called thermals.

White-Tailed Deer flash their white tails as a warning signal when they sense danger.

Yellow-Bellied Marmots whistle loudly to warn others of predators like eagles or coyotes.

Zebra Swallowtail Butterflies have long tails that look like a leaf, helping them hide from predators.

What Do You Know?

Use these questions to spark curiosity and conversation. Talk about details you notice in the photos and what you've learned together from *Would You Believe?* facts and other sources.

1. Which North American animal surprised you the most? What about that animal is most interesting to you?

2. Which animal do you think would be easiest to spot in the wild? Which animal do you think would be hardest to spot? Why?

3. Which North American animal would you want to see up close? Why?

4. How do you think animals like coyotes, elk, and quail stay safe by living in groups?

5. Which animals have horns or antlers? How are these animals different from each other? How are they the same?

6. Some animals hibernate, or sleep, in the winter. Why do you think they do that?

7. What do you think animals that live in forests might have in common?

8. Which North American animals do you think live in groups? Which ones might live alone? What clues helped you decide?

9. Pick a North American animal. How do you think it protects itself from danger?

10. If you made up a new North American animal, where would it live and what would it eat?

11. How do you think an animal's habitat effects what it eats or how it behaves?

12. If you could be one North American animal for a day, which one would you choose? Why?

How Do You Say It?

American Black Bear
(uh-MAIR-ih-kuhn BLAK bair)

Bald Eagle (BAWLD EE-guhl)

Coyote (ky-OH-tee)

Dall Sheep (DAWL SHEEP)

Elk (ELK)

Fox (FAHKS)

Grizzly Bear (GRIZ-lee bair)

Hawk (HAWK)

Indigo Bunting (IN-duh-goh BUN-ting)

Jackrabbit (JAK-rab-it)

Killdeer (KIL-deer)

Lynx (LINKS)

Moose (MOOS)

North American Porcupine
(NORTH uh-MAIR-ih-kuhn POR-kyoo-pine)

Opossum (Virginia Opossum)
(uh-POSS-uhm [vur-JIN-yuh uh-POSS-uhm])

Pronghorn (PRONG-horn)

Quail (KWAYL)

Raccoon (ra-KOON)

Skunk (SKUNK)

Turkey (TUR-kee)

Uinta Ground Squirrel
(yoo-IN-tuh GROUND SKWUR-uhl)

Vulture (Turkey Vulture)
(VUL-chur [TUR-kee VUL-chur])

White-Tailed Deer (WYT-TAYLD DEER)

Yellow-Bellied Marmot
(YEL-oh BEL-eed MAR-muht)

Zebra Swallowtail Butterfly
(ZEE-bruh SWOL-oh-tayl BUT-er-fly)

Sources Alaska Department of Fish and Game (https://www.adfg.alaska.gov); All About Birds: Cornell Lab of Ornithology (https://www.allaboutbirds.org/guide); American Museum of Natural History: OLogy: The Science Website for Kids (https://www.amnh.org/explore/ology); BBC Earth (https://www.bbcearth.com); Birds of the World: Cornell Lab of Ornithology (https://birdsoftheworld.org); Butterflies and Moths of North America (https://www.butterfliesandmoths.org); California Department of Fish and Wildlife (https://wildlife.ca.gov); National Audubon Society (https://www.audubon.org); National Geographic Kids (https://kids.nationalgeographic.com/animals); National Wildlife Federation (https://www.nwf.org/Educational-Resources/Wildlife-Guide); Nature Conservancy of Canada (https://www.natureconservancy.ca); North American Nature (https://northamerican-nature.com); PBS Nature (https://www.pbs.org/wnet/nature/coyote); Rocky Mountain Elk Foundation (https://www.rmef.org/elk-facts); San Diego Zoo Kids: San Diego Zoo Wildlife Alliance (https://kids.sandiegozoo.org/animals); Smithsonian Institution: National Museum of Natural History (https://naturalhistory.si.edu); Smithsonian Magazine (https://www.smithsonianmag.com); Smithsonian's National Zoo and Conservation Biology Institute (https://nationalzoo.si.edu/animals); U.S. Forest Service: Wildlife & Fish (https://www.fs.usda.gov); U.S. National Park Service (https://www.nps.gov/subjects/watchingwildlife); University of Utah (https://nhmu.utah.edu); Utah Division of Wildlife Resources (https://wildlife.utah.gov); World Wildlife Fund: Species Directory (https://www.worldwildlife.org/species)

More animals.
More fun.
More to explore.